W9-DHS-402

CAST IRON KITCHEN

CAST IRON KITCHEN

OVER 50 FRESH, NEW RECIPES

JESSECA HALLOWS

AUTHOR OF *FOILED!: EASY, TASTY, TIN FOIL MEALS*

FRONT TABLE BOOKS | AN IMPRINT OF CEDAR FORT, INC. | SPRINGVILLE, UTAH

© 2018 Jesseca Hallows
All rights reserved.

No part of this book may be reproduced in any form whatsoever, whether by graphic, visual, electronic, film, microfilm, tape recording, or any other means, without prior written permission of the publisher, except in the case of brief passages embodied in critical reviews and articles.

The opinions and views expressed herein belong solely to the authors and do not necessarily represent the opinions or views of Cedar Fort, Inc. Permission for the use of sources, graphics, and photos is also solely the responsibility of the authors.

ISBN 13: 978-1-4621-1969-1

Published by Front Table Books, an imprint of Cedar Fort, Inc.
2373 W. 700 S., Springville, UT 84663
Distributed by Cedar Fort, Inc., www.cedarfort.com

LIBRARY OF CONGRESS CATALOGING-IN-PUBLICATION DATA

Names: Hallows, Jesseca, 1987-
Title: Cast iron kitchen : over 50 fresh, new recipes / Jesseca Hallows.
Description: Springville, Utah : Front Table Books, An imprint of Cedar Fort, Inc., [2017] | Includes index.
Identifiers: LCCN 2017052657 (print) | LCCN 2017053802 (ebook) | ISBN
  9781462127412 (epub, pdf, mobi) | ISBN 9781462119691 (perfect bound : alk. paper)
Subjects: LCSH: Skillet cooking. | Dutch oven cooking. | Cast-iron. | LCGFT: Cookbooks.
Classification: LCC TX840.S55 (ebook) | LCC TX840.S55 H35 2017 (print) | DDC 641.7/7--dc23
LC record available at https://lccn.loc.gov/2017052657

Cover design by Priscilla Chaves
Page design by M. Shaun McMurdie
Cover design © 2018 Cedar Fort, Inc.
Edited by Erica Myers

Printed in the United States of America

10 9 8 7 6 5 4 3 2 1

Printed on acid-free paper

DEDICATION

This book is dedicated to my brother and sister who didn't think it was cool to publish a book. I made every recipe extra delicious to spite you.

CONTENTS

47   DINNER

ACKNOWLEDGMENTS

To my husband, saying you are my better half is an understatement. Thank you for taste testing countless meals and putting up with my emotional meltdowns when recipes have failed. You have always been there to lift me up, wash my dishes, and encourage me to keep going when I'm ready to give up.

To Daxton, If it wasn't for your constant companionship in the kitchen this book would not be a reality. You are the mac to my cheese, the PB to my J, and the best hugger in times of frustration. Never change.

Special thanks to Karina for giving me expert advice as well as being my constant go-to for new recipe inspiration. You are one of a kind and someone I am happy to know and love.

INTRODUCTION

I grew up watching my grandmother cook with cast iron cookware and it was a beautiful thing. She was always so majestic in the kitchen. Watching her whip up a fresh batch of tortillas was like watching my very own live version of Julia Child, minus the butter. She had this gorgeous cast iron piece that was part of her original wood stove. It was so beautiful and heavily used. She would always tell me that it spread extra love into her food. I've always kept that saying with me and like to think I sprinkle love into each of my recipes.

In this book, you will find everything from savory breakfasts to sweet treats. My goal is to share how versatile your pans can be and help you transition them into your daily users! Don't let cast iron be intimidating. Embrace the wonderful kitchen staple and get cooking.

Jesseca

TYPES OF CAST IRON

I could talk for days about the history of cast iron, but I'll try to keep this brief. Let's chit chat about the different types you will see. Cast iron comes in two different styles: bare and enamel coated. I happen to own both and am here to tell you that they both rock. I know what you're thinking: I must not be a true cast iron user. But the truth is they both have wonderful aspects.

Let's start by talking about bare pans. These are the pans you'll see in the camping section of almost every store. They come without any covering and need to be seasoned (though some do come preseasoned). They are typically more cost friendly, which is always a good place to start. They are durable and could potentially last a lifetime if cared for correctly.

The second, enamel coated, is a little higher on the price list. I own a dutch oven version, and it is my favorite pan. They do NOT need to be seasoned, since they are non stick right out of the box! How great is that? These don't tend to last as long but won't break down quickly if well cared for.

They are both great and either will work for ALL recipes in this book unless specifically stated.

QUICK CLEANING GUIDE

A quick internet search will show you about one million different ways to clean your cast iron. I'm not saying my way is the only way, but it's the way I've used and it works. You can follow these steps or use whatever way you find that works for you!

1. While your pan is still hot, gently scrub with a rag or stiff brush. Rinse with hot water.

2. Dry completely. I like to set mine on the stove and turn it on medium heat for 5 to 10 minutes.

3. Wipe with oil.

That's it! If you have a particularly stubborn build up, use coarse salt as your scrubbing assistant. This can help break down any leftover residue. Make sure you never soak your pan(s) or wash them in the dishwasher.

SEASONING

Most cast iron pans you purchase come pre-seasoned. In the off chance that yours does not, or you accidentally scrub off some of the seasoning, you'll need to reseason. This is the one and only time you will hear me say that you will use soap on your skillet. If you aren't seasoning, just don't do it. It's a bad idea. This one and only time I give you permission. Follow the steps below for perfect seasoning.

1. Wash your pan with hot soapy water and dry thoroughly.

2. Spread oil (I like flaxseed oil) over the inside and outside of your pan.

3. Bake upside down at 325 degrees for 1 hour.

4. Wait for the pan to cool completely before removing from the oven.

Easy peasy, right? You are now ready to move on to the next step, COOKING!

HOW TO STORE YOUR CAST IRON

I used to store my cast iron in an empty pantry shelf close to the sink. It seemed to work well for a long time but it turns out not prepping a bit before caused one giant headache when I reached for my very much loved pan and found it rusted. My heart sank to my stomach and I thought my beloved pan was ruined forever (more on that in the next section). Turns out there are just a few easy storing tips you should follow in order to keep your pans in tip-top shape!

1. Clean and dry your pans thoroughly. Follow the previous steps to clean your cast iron making sure to dry completely. Leaving any additional moisture will quickly cause your pans to rust leaving you with a mess.

2. Always season before storing. Giving your cast iron the proper seasoning is key to keeping it non-stick and new. A quick wipe of oil will do the trick.

3. Store in a dry place. We have a wonderful pantry far from the sink that we like to keep our cast iron in. Try to avoid any spots that tend to be more moist or could potentially have a higher chance of water leaks.

4. Layer with paper towels. It might sound weird, but if you plan on stacking your cast iron it's a great idea to add a paper towel between each piece. This will help absorb any moisture as well as protect your pan from any dings or scrapes.

You know the warming drawer under your oven? The one that is almost never used? We find that it's the perfect place to store our cast iron collection. The warm oven keeps moisture away and you are able to fit many different sizes!

HOW TO SAVE A RUSTED CAST IRON PIECE

Imagine if you will, you reach into the pantry to grab your favorite cast iron pan only to find it rusted and ruined. Your heart sinks at the thought of needing to replace the pan and losing one of your favorite kitchen pieces. The good news is that with a little elbow grease you can save the pan and have it looking good as new in no time! Follow the steps below to help clean and repair your damaged pan.

1. Scrub your pan with soap and steel wool. This goes against everything I have told you when it comes to caring for your cast iron, but it's ok in this one instance. Scrub your pan in hot water with soap until all traces of the rust are removed.

2. Dry completely. I always towel dry and place on a hot burner for 5-7 minutes to ensure there is no left behind moisture.

3. Follow the steps to seasoning your cast iron. Just like that, you have a restored pan ready to use!

BREAKFAST

SAUSAGE GRAVY

If you have to pick only one recipe from this book to make, let it be this sausage gravy. The ingredients are minimal, and you still get outstanding flavor. Smother fresh buttermilk biscuits with the gravy and top with an egg for the perfect savory breakfast. Bonus, you get a great seasoning layer on your skillet!

SERVES 6-8

1 lb. **breakfast sausage**

2 Tbsp. **butter**

½ cup **flour**

4 cups **whole milk**

¾ tsp. **salt**

1-2 tsp. fresh **cracked pepper**

1. Heat a 12-inch skillet over medium heat 10 minutes or until warmed.

2. Add the sausage and cook until crumbled and browned.

3. Stir in the butter and flour until all of the clumps have dissolved. Slowly whisk in the milk. Simmer 8–10 minutes or until thickened.

4. Season with salt and pepper.

TIPS

I prefer spicy breakfast sausage or maple with this recipe, but it will work with any breakfast sausage variety.

Start with just 1 teaspoon of pepper and add more to taste.

BUTTERMILK BISCUITS

I have made dozens of biscuits in my life, and these are by far my favorite! I've made them time and time again and am never disappointed. The secret is to work the dough as little as possible and keep things cold.

SERVES 5

2 cups **flour**

1 Tbsp. **baking powder**

½ tsp. **salt**

½ cup **butter**, cold and cut into small cubes

1 cup + 2 Tbsp. **buttermilk**

1. Place a 10-inch skillet in the oven and turn temperature to 425 degrees.

2. While that is heating, combine the flour, baking powder, and salt into a chilled bowl. Cut the butter in using a chilled pastry cutter or two knives until the butter resembles small crumbles.

3. Gently stir in the 1 cup buttermilk until dough just forms. Transfer to a lightly floured work surface and pat down to 1-inch thick rectangle. Fold into thirds.

4. Pat dough into 1-inch thick rectangle and fold one more time. Gently pat one last time and use a round cutter to cut your biscuits.

5. Transfer the biscuits to the warmed pan, brush with the 2 tablespoons of buttermilk, and bake 15 minutes or until golden brown.

TIPS

Chill your bowl, pastry cutter, and butter for 20 minutes before you start to work to help your biscuits stay cold.

Grease your pan with butter or oil before adding the biscuits if not well seasoned.

HUEVOS RANCHEROS

I grew up thinking homemade refried beans and tortillas were considered a full meal. My grandma always had a fresh batch made when we came to visit, and we loved eating them on everything (and I mean everything). Breakfast was no exception! This Huevos Rancheros is as close to authentic as we got and one of my favorites to this day.

SERVES 2

½ cup **refried beans**

2 Tbsp. **enchilada sauce**

2 Tbsp. diced **green chilies**

2 Tbsp. **oil**

2 corn **tortillas**

2 large **eggs**

½ cup shredded **pepper jack cheese**

¼ cup **picco**

fresh **cilantro**

1. Stir together the refried beans, enchilada sauce, and green chilies in a small pot. Bring to a simmer and set aside.

2. Heat the oil in an 8-inch skillet. Fry the tortillas 1 minute on each side until firm. Place on your plates and spread each with ½ of the bean mixture.

3. Use the oil to fry the two eggs over medium and transfer to your prepared tortillas. Top with cheese and pico and sprinkle with cilantro.

TIP
Add additional oil before frying the eggs if necessary.

BREAKFAST POTATOES

Sometimes less is more and that is the case with these potatoes! My mom used to whip up a version of these served with her Spicy Indian Chili, and all of us kids would fight over the crispy pieces. Since then, I have adapted a version that is oh so perfect as a savory side to any meal! Try it topped with an egg or alongside my Huevos Rancheros.

SERVES 4

3 Tbsp. **butter or oil**

3 large **Yukon Gold potatoes**, cut into small cubes

1 tsp. **salt**

¼ tsp. **pepper**

¼ cup diced **onion**

2 slices of uncooked **bacon**, diced (optional)

1. Heat a 10-inch cast iron skillet over medium-high heat.

2. Add the butter to the pan and allow to melt. Lower the temperature to medium and stir in the potatoes, making sure to cover them in the melted butter.

3. Spread into an even layer and sprinkle with salt and pepper.

4. Cook the potatoes for ten minutes, stirring only a few times.

5. Add the diced onion and bacon if using to the pan, stirring to combine. Cook an additional 8–10 minutes or until the potatoes are crisp and the onions are translucent.

TIP
Make sure your potatoes are very dry before adding them to your pan. This helps them get crisp.

CINNAMON TWISTS

Easy is the name of this game. I have been using puff pastry to whip up these cinnamon twists for years. Imagine a croissant meets cinnamon roll. That is the best description for this treat. The crisp outer layer makes the perfect container for the sweet filling.

SERVES 3-5

1 sheet **puff pastry**

2 Tbsp. **butter**, melted

¾ cup **brown sugar**

2 Tbsp. **ground cinnamon**

2 oz. **cream cheese**

2 Tbsp. **butter**

½ cup **powdered sugar**

½ tsp. **pure vanilla extract**

1. Spray a 10-inch cast iron skillet with nonstick spray and set aside.

2. Bring your puff pastry to room temperature and roll out on a lightly floured work surface.

3. Brush pastry with butter.

4. Mix together both the brown sugar and cinnamon. Sprinkle over your dough.

5. Slice into triangle shapes and gently roll into a croissant form.

6. Bake at 350 degrees for 20 minutes.

7. While the twists are baking whisk together the cream cheese, butter, powdered sugar, and vanilla extract. Drizzle over your pastries and enjoy!

SKILLET CAKES (PANCAKES)

I've got a seven-year-old with a serious sweet tooth, so anything with the word cake in it that is an acceptable form of breakfast gets five stars in his book. These pancakes are fluffy perfection and practically melt in your mouth! The secret is using a cast iron skillet and lots of butter!

SERVES 4

1½ cups **flour**

2 Tbsp. **granulated sugar**

1½ tsp. **baking powder**

¾ tsp. **baking soda**

¼ tsp. **salt**

1½ cups **buttermilk**

¼ cup **whole milk**

2 large **eggs**

3 Tbsp. **butter**, melted

½ tsp. **pure vanilla extract**

1. Whisk together the flour, sugar, baking powder, baking soda, and salt in a large bowl and set aside.

2. Combine the buttermilk, milk, eggs, butter, and vanilla in a large measuring cup and mix to combine. Pour and fold into your dry ingredients until just combined, being careful not to over mix.

3. Scoop ½ cup of your batter onto a preheated skillet. Cook over medium-low heat until bubbles begin to form. Flip and cook an additional 2–3 minutes or until golden brown.

4. Serve with syrup, jam, or fresh fruit.

TIPS
Use room temperature ingredients for fluffy pancakes. I take my eggs and milk out of the refrigerator 20 minutes before starting.

Do not over mix the batter. This recipe turns out best if you gently fold the ingredients together.

Clarified butter is what I use when greasing my pan. It tends to brown less quickly and gives my pancakes a beautiful golden color.

PUFF PANCAKE

If you haven't experienced the magic of a puff pancake, you are truly missing out. Toss all of the ingredients into a blender and pour into a preheated skillet filled with melted butter and let the oven do the rest! My family loves this covered in syrup, but it's also delicious with fresh fruit!

SERVES 4

4 Tbsp. **butter**

3 large **eggs**

½ cup **flour**

½ cup **whole milk**

1 Tbsp. **granulated sugar**

¼ tsp. **cinnamon**

¼ tsp. **pure vanilla extract**

1. Add butter to the inside of a 10-inch cast iron skillet and place in a cold oven. Preheat to 375 degrees.

2. Combine the eggs, flour, milk, sugar, cinnamon, and vanilla to a blender. Pulse until smooth.

3. Remove the skillet from the oven, making sure to use oven mitts. Pour the batter directly over the butter. No need to stir.

4. Bake 25 minutes or until the middle is set and the sides are puffed over the edge of your pan.

TIP
Add fresh fruit to your pancake or serve with warm maple syrup.

BLUEBERRY BREAKFAST CAKE

I adore coffee cake (or really any cake for that matter). This recipe is one of my family's all-time favorites because it is so deliciously easy to make. I've been known to swap the blueberries for other in-season fruit on occasion with wonderful results, so don't be afraid to play around with different flavors!

SERVES 12

FOR THE CAKE

2 cups **flour**

2 tsp. **baking powder**

½ tsp. **salt**

1 cup **sugar**

4 Tbsp. **butter,** melted and slightly cooled

⅓ cup **sour cream**

1 large **egg**

½ cup **buttermilk**

1 tsp. **pure vanilla extract**

1 cup **blueberries**

FOR THE TOPPING

⅓ cup **flour**

½ cup **brown sugar**

½ tsp. **ground cinnamon**

¼ cup **butter,** softened

1. Preheat your oven to 375 degrees. Grease the inside of a 10-inch skillet with butter or non-stick spray and set aside.

2. Combine 2 cups of flour, baking powder, salt, and sugar in a medium sized bowl. Whisk and set aside.

3. Stir together the butter, sour cream, egg, buttermilk, and vanilla in a large measuring cup. Gently mix into the dry ingredients until fully incorporated. Fold in the blueberries and transfer to your prepared skillet.

4. For the topping; whisk together ⅓ cup of flour with the brown sugar and cinnamon. Cut in the butter until coarse crumbs have formed. Sprinkle over the top of your cake.

5. Bake for 40 minutes or until a toothpick comes out clean.

TIP
Try substituting cherries for the blueberries and almond extract for the vanilla for another great variation.

BREAKFAST SCRAMBLE

Savory breakfast lovers rejoice! This breakfast scramble is a family favorite that is made often in our home. While one of the three of us loves to start the day on a sweet note the other two prefer to start it with BACON. Serve this easy recipe with a side of toast or wrapped in a tortilla.

SERVES 4

2 Tbsp. **butter**, divided

½ medium **onion**, chopped

6 slices uncooked **bacon**, diced

5 large **eggs**

2 Tbsp. **whole milk**

½ tsp. **salt**

¼ tsp. **pepper**

1 cup shredded **cheddar cheese**

1. Preheat a 10-inch skillet over medium heat. Add 1 tablespoon of butter with the onions and bacon. Sauté until the onion is translucent.

2. Whisk the eggs with the milk, salt, and pepper together in a medium measuring cup.

3. Add the remaining 1 tablespoon of butter to the bacon and pour the eggs over the top. Cook, making sure to turn several times with a spatula until the eggs are set. Top with cheese.

MOUNTAIN MAN BREAKFAST CASSEROLE

This day starting meal is perfect for feeding a crowd. We often make it while camping or even to enjoy on Christmas morning. The crispy potatoes, eggs, and veggies give you a full belly with lots of flavor.

SERVES 6

2 Tbsp. **oil**

½ lb. **breakfast sausage**

½ small chopped **onion**

2 **garlic cloves**, minced

¼ **red pepper**, chopped

¼ **green pepper**, chopped

3 cups frozen shredded **hash browns**

6 large **eggs**

½ tsp. **salt**

¼ tsp. **pepper**

2 Tbsp. **green salsa**

2 Tbsp. **sour cream**

2 cups **cheddar cheese**, divided

1. Place a 12-inch skillet in a cold oven and preheat it to 350 degrees.

2. Once warmed, place the skillet on the stove over medium heat.

3. Heat the oil in your pan. Add the sausage and onion. Cook until browned and stir in the red and green pepper and hash browns.

4. Continue to cook until the potatoes are browned and slightly crisp.

5. In a small bowl, whisk together the eggs, salt, pepper, salsa, sour cream, and 1 cup of cheese. Pour evenly over your potato mixture.

6. Bake for 35 minutes. Sprinkle with remaining cheese and bake 5 minutes more.

BAKED EGGS

THESE eggs! Out of all the recipes in the breakfast section, this one is my personal favorite. It's one I make frequently and is easily adaptable. Top with avocado, a dash of hot sauce, or even some chopped green onion to give these eggs a little pop of flavor.

SERVES 2

½ cup **canned diced tomatoes with green chilies**, drained

2 slices **bacon**, cooked and crumbled

3 large **eggs**

½ tsp. **salt**

¼ tsp. **pepper**

2 Tbsp. crumbled **feta cheese** (optional)

1. Place an 8-inch skillet in a cold oven. Heat to 375 degrees.

2. Carefully remove the skillet from the oven. Mist with non-stick spray or grease with butter.

3. Evenly spread the tomatoes into the pan and sprinkle with bacon. Carefully crack eggs over the top, making sure not to break the yolks. Sprinkle with salt and pepper.

4. Place in the oven and bake for 10–15 minutes or until the whites are set. Sprinkle with cheese.

TIP
Bring your eggs to room temperature before baking. This helps them set quicker in the oven.

BREAKFAST HASH

I teetered back and forth on if I should share this breakfast hash or homemade hash browns. I asked for a vote from my family and there was an overwhelming response. Everyone said Breakfast Hash is a must make as an easy side dish or main course!

SERVES 1-2

3 Tbsp. **butter or oil**

3 large **Yukon Gold potatoes**, cut into small cubes

1 tsp. **salt**

¼ tsp. **pepper**

¼ cup diced **onion**

¼ cup diced **green or red pepper** (optional)

2 slices of uncooked **bacon**, diced

1 **egg**, fried

1. Heat the butter in a 10-inch skillet over medium heat.

2. Once the butter is hot add the onion, pepper, and bacon. Cook one minute, or until the onions are just beginning to soften.

3. Add the potatoes and season with salt and pepper. Reduce the heat and continue to cook for 10 minutes. Add the bacon and continue to cook 10 minutes or until the potatoes are golden and the onions have caramelized, making sure to stir frequently.

4. Top with a fried egg and enjoy.

SWEET POTATO BREAKFAST HASH

SERVES 2

1-2 Tbsp. **olive oil**

1 large **sweet potato**, peeled and cut into ½-inch cubes

¼ **green pepper**, diced

¼ **red pepper**, diced

¼ small **onion**, diced

2 cloves **garlic**

½ cup packed **fresh spinach**

2-3 large **eggs**

salt and pepper to taste

hot sauce or salsa (optional)

1. Preheat your oven to 400 degrees.

2. Heat your olive oil in a 9-inch skillet over medium heat. Add your sweet potatoes and cook 5 minutes, stirring occasionally.

3. Stir in the green pepper, red pepper, and onion. Continue to cook an additional 5 minutes or until all of the vegetables are soft. Stir in your garlic and spinach and season with salt and pepper.

4. Crack 2–3 eggs over your vegetables. Season with salt and pepper to taste. Bake 10–15 minutes or until the eggs are just set. Make sure to watch closely to avoid overcooking.

5. Serve with hot sauce or salsa if desired.

PERFECT FRENCH TOAST

The addition of vanilla bean adds a touch of elegance to this dish! Those beautiful specks coat each slice and the honey helps add a touch of caramelization. Serve warm with fresh fruit, a dust of powdered sugar, or warm syrup!

SERVES 4

4 large **eggs**

½ cup **whole milk**

1 Tbsp. **honey**

½ tsp. **ground cinnamon**

1½ tsp. **vanilla bean paste**

3 Tbsp. **butter**, divided

8 slices thick cut **bread**

1. Preheat a large skillet over medium heat.

2. Whisk together the eggs, milk, honey, cinnamon, and vanilla bean paste in a large shallow bowl.

3. Place 1 tablespoon of butter in your heated skillet and swirl to cover.

4. Dip one slice of bread in your egg mixture, making sure to flip and coat both sides.

5. Transfer the slice to your skillet and cook 2–3 minutes on each side or until golden.

6. Repeat with the remaining slices, adding the rest of the butter to the skillet as needed.

APPLE CINNAMON BAKED OATMEAL

Warning! While baking this oatmeal your home will smell delicious. You will start craving more and more fall recipes, and you will not have leftovers!

SERVES 8

2⅔ cup **rolled oats**

½ cup **brown sugar**

2 tsp. **ground cinnamon**

½ tsp. **salt**

4 Tbsp. **butter**

3 cups **whole milk**

2 cups chopped **apples**, cut into ½-inch cubes

1 cup **walnuts or pecans** (optional)

1. Place a 9-inch skillet in a cold oven. Preheat to 350 degrees.

2. Combine all of the ingredients into a mixing bowl. Stir until fully incorporated and carefully transfer to your heated skillet.

3. Bake 40 minutes or until set and a majority of the liquid is absorbed.

TIPS

Serve warm or cold in a bowl with milk.

Try substituting almond or coconut milk for a change in flavor.

CORNMEAL CAKES

I grew up loving cornmeal for breakfast. When my mom's side of the family would get together we would all enjoy "mush" for breakfast which is basically a giant overnight pancake made completely with cornmeal. This recipe is my interpretation of that nostalgic breakfast. Serve it as is or toss in some blueberries of a great complimentary flavor!

SERVES 4

1 cup + 2 Tbsp. **flour**

⅓ cup **yellow cornmeal**

2 Tbsp. **granulated sugar**

1 tsp. **baking powder**

½ tsp. **baking soda**

½ tsp. **salt**

2 large **eggs**

¾ cup **plain yogurt**

¾ cup **milk**

¼ cup **oil** (I use coconut, but vegetable would work too)

1 tsp. **vanilla extract**

1. Whisk together the flour, cornmeal, sugar, baking powder, baking soda, and salt in a large bowl.

2. Combine the eggs, yogurt, milk, oil, and vanilla in a measuring cup. Whisk to combine and fold into the dry ingredients until just combined.

3. Heat a skillet over low/medium heat. Grease with non-stick spray or butter and scoop ⅓ cup of the batter into your pan. Cook 2–3 minutes or until bubbles begin to form on the surface and flip. Cook an additional 2–3 minutes or until browned.

TIP
Serve with honey butter, syrup, or berries.

DINNER

PERFECT PAN-SEARED STEAK

This recipe. It's "the one" for me. Whenever I have to choose a meal I always tend to lean pretty heavily into the red meat category. It wasn't until recently when my little guy decided he too loved steak that I started to cook it a little more frequently. You will not believe how simple this dish is and will find yourself making it time and time again.

SERVES 1-2

1 thick cut **steak**
(about 2 lbs.)

Salt and pepper
to taste

1. Remove your steak* from the refrigerator about 20 minutes before cooking and allow to come to room temperature.

2. Heat a 12-inch skillet over medium-high heat until smoking hot.**

3. Sprinkle your steak with salt and pepper on both sides. Place in your heated skillet and cook 4 minutes. Flip and continue to cook an additional 2–5 minutes or until desired doneness is reached.

* For this recipe I like to use a rib-eye, New York strip, and filet.

**This recipe causes quite a bit of smoke. Make sure you open a window and start a fan before cooking.

THE BEST MACARONI AND CHEESE

My love for cheese runs deep. So it would only make sense I'd add my all-time favorite macaroni recipe to this book! There are not one, not two, but THREE different varieties of cheese combined to make this recipe one you will never forget. Kid and husband approved.

SERVES 6-8

¾ cup **butter**

½ tsp. **salt**

½ tsp. **pepper**

½ tsp. **dry mustard**

¼ cup **flour**

2 cups **whole milk**

3 cups shredded **sharp cheddar cheese**, divided

2 cups shredded **pepper jack cheese**

¼ cup **sour cream**

2 cups **elbow macaroni**, cooked al dente

1. Preheat the oven to 350 degrees.

2. Melt the butter in a medium saucepan over medium heat. Whisk in the salt, pepper, dry mustard, and flour. Cook 2 minutes while continuing to whisk.

3. Slowly pour in milk. Bring to a simmer. Cook until just thickening and remove from the heat.

4. Stir in both cheeses and sour cream. Once melted add your macaroni. Pour into a deep 9-inch cast iron pan.

5. Bake 20–25 minutes or until bubbly and slightly browned on top.

LASAGNA SKILLET

This one is for my pasta-loving friends. I've taken the classic pasta dish and simplified it with this one-pan dinner. It's a snap to whip up and put on your table in no time.

SERVES 6

1 Tbsp. **olive oil**

1 lb. **Italian sausage or ground beef**

2 cloves **garlic**

1 (28-oz.) can **diced tomatoes** (I use Italian seasoned)

1 (8-oz.) can **tomato sauce**

1 Tbsp. **sugar**

¼ tsp. **red pepper flakes**

1 Tbsp. **Italian seasoning**

1 tsp. **salt**

½ tsp. **pepper**

12 oz. **bow tie pasta**

½ cup **water**

1 cup shredded **mozzarella** (optional)

½ cup **ricotta**

1. Preheat oven to 350 degrees.

2. Heat oil in a 12-inch skillet. Add the sausage and cook until browned. Stir in the garlic and cook one minute more.

3. Mix in the diced tomatoes, tomato sauce, sugar, red pepper flakes, Italian seasoning, salt, pepper, and pasta. Pour the water over the top and cover.

4. Simmer 20–25 minutes or until the pasta is tender.

5. Top with mozzarella and ricotta. Place in the oven and heat 10 minutes until the cheese is melted.

CHEAT GARLIC KNOTS

I'm a sucker for garlic AND easy recipes. Luckily this side is both of those things. I'm taking pre-prepared bread dough and adding my own special twist making these the perfect side dish to any pizza or pasta dinner!

SERVES 6-8

3 Tbsp. **grated parmesan cheese**

½ tsp. **salt**

1½ tsp. **garlic powder**

½ tsp. **oregano**

½ tsp. **basil**

½ tsp. **parsley**

12 **frozen rolls**

¼ cup **butter**, melted

1. Whisk the parmesan, salt, garlic powder, oregano, basil, and parsley in a small bowl. Set aside.

2. Remove rolls from the freezer and leave out until just thawed.

3. Roll into 4-inch long ropes and tie into knots. Place on a greased 9-inch pan and allow to rise until doubled.

4. Preheat oven to 350 degrees.

5. Bake for 8–10 minutes or until golden on top.

6. Brush with melted butter and sprinkle with garlic seasoning.

MARGARITA CHICKEN

This tasty chicken dish is a great way to spice up your go-to weeknight meal. The secret to the bold flavor is in the cilantro-packed marinade. You're left with a savory dish sure to please the entire family!

SERVES 2-4

½ cup + 1 Tbsp. **olive oil**

⅓ cup chopped **cilantro**

1 Tbsp. **ground pepper**

1 tsp. **garlic powder**

½ tsp. **onion powder**

¼ cup **margarita mix**, non-alcoholic

¼ cup **lime juice**

2 Tbsp. **fresh orange juice**

2 Tbsp. **orange zest**

1 tsp. **garlic**

1 Tbsp. **apricot preserves**

4 **chicken breast halves**

tomatoes and lime wedges

1. Combine ½ cup olive oil, cilantro, pepper, garlic powder, onion powder, margarita mix, lime juice, orange juice, orange zest, garlic, and apricot preserves in a large Ziploc bag. Add your chicken breasts, seal closed, and refrigerate at least 4 hours (but ideally 24 hours).

2. Preheat your oven to 400 degrees.

3. Heat 1 tablespoon olive oil in a cast iron or oven-safe pan over medium-high heat. Add the chicken and cook 2 minutes on each side or until just browned.

4. Transfer to the oven and cook 15–20 minutes or until the chicken reaches 165 degrees.

5. Let rest 10 minutes before serving.

SKILLET PIZZA

Pizza night takes on an entirely new meaning when you are preparing in cast iron! Use the toppings I suggest or get creative and add your favorite go-to recipes! It's a fun and fresh take on the classic dinner.

SERVES 3

1 premade **pizza dough**

2 Tbsp. **flour**

2 Tbsp. **cornmeal**

¼ cup **pizza sauce**

Fresh mozzarella, shredded

Any additional toppings of your choosing

1. Preheat your oven to 500 degrees.

2. Place a 12-inch skillet over the burner on medium-high heat.

3. While your pan is heating, carefully stretch your dough into a round.

4. Sprinkle your hot pan with flour and cornmeal. Carefully place your dough into the pan making sure to gently press it into the corners and pull the sides up forming your crust. Cook 7 minutes or just until bubbles start to form.

5. Spread pizza sauce followed by the mozzarella onto the pizza.

6. Add any additional toppings.

7. Bake 10 minutes or until cheese is melted.

CHEESY GARLIC PULL-APART BREAD

Like my garlic knots, this cheesy bread is the perfect side to any meal. You are sure to win over even the pickiest eater with this family favorite.

SERVES 6

½ cup melted **butter**, cooled slightly

1 Tbsp. **italian seasoning**

5-7 cloves **garlic**, minced

2 (10-oz.) cans **refrigerated biscuits**

⅓ cup shredded fresh **parmesan cheese**

1. Place a 9-inch skillet in a cold oven. Heat to 350 degrees.

2. While your pan is heating combine the butter, Italian seasoning, and garlic in a large Ziploc bag.

3. Quarter the biscuits and add to the butter mixture. Shake until well coated and carefully add to your heated pan.

4. Bake 15–20 minutes or until lightly browned. Sprinkle with cheese and bake an additional 2–3 minutes or until just melted.

TATER TOT CASSEROLE

If you asked my seven year old which recipe from this book was his favorite, hands down this would be it. We make Tatertot Casserole way too often and it never gets old.

SERVES 4-6

1 lb. **ground beef**

1 Tbsp. **seasoning salt**

1 can **cream of mushroom soup**

½ cup **milk**

1 Tbsp. **Worcestershire sauce**

3 cups **tater tots**

1 cup shredded **cheddar cheese**

1. Preheat your oven to 425 degrees.

2. Combine your ground beef and seasoning salt in a 12-inch skillet. Cook over medium heat until the meat is browned and onion is soft.

3. Stir in the mushroom soup, milk, and worcestershire sauce. Top with tater tots and bake 20 minutes.

4. Sprinkle with cheese and cook an additional 5 minutes or until the cheese is melted.

TIP
Stir your favorite veggie right into the meat mixture before adding the tatertots.

INCREDIBLY SIMPLE CHICKEN FAJITAS

You know those super simple recipes you seem to reach for on those nights when you're just too busy to think? This is that recipe for me. It comes together in a snap and all of the magic happens in the oven! Using a well seasoned (and loved) skillet helps give these fajitas bold flavor.

SERVES 4

½ large **onion**

½ **red pepper**

½ **green pepper**

2 large **chicken breasts**

1-2 Tbsp. **olive oil**

1 Tbsp. **fajita seasoning**
(taco seasoning works
in a pinch)

Tortillas

Sour cream

Salsa

1. Place a 12-inch skillet in a cold oven and preheat to 400 degrees.

2. While your oven is preheating cut your onion, peppers, and chicken into thin strips. Toss with olive oil and fajita seasoning.

3. Carefully remove your pan from the oven. Add your chicken mixture and continue to bake 20 minutes or until your chicken is cooked through.

4. Serve inside of your tortillas with sour cream and salsa or your favorite toppings.

TIPS

Cut your chicken and peppers 1-3 days in advance for easy meal prep.

This recipe can also be done stove top.

FLOUR TORTILLAS

When I was a little girl, I could always count on my grandma to keep her pantry well stocked with homemade tortillas. It was a mad dash into the kitchen between my sisters and me to see who would get first pick. Those memories are ones I will cherish forever and a tradition I keep going with my eight-year-old.

MAKES ABOUT EIGHT 10-INCH TORTILLAS

4 cups **flour**

1 tsp. **salt**

2 tsp. **baking powder**

2 Tbsp. **shortening**

1½ cups **hot water**

1. Whisk together the flour, salt, and baking powder in a medium bowl. Cut in the shortening with a pastry blender, or your fingers, until dough is crumbly.

2. Slowly stir in the hot water and mix until just combined. Turn onto a lightly floured surface and knead 3–4 times or until smooth.

3. Divide your dough into 8 equal pieces. Roll into a very thin round tortilla shape.

4. Cook on a preheated skillet until lightly golden on each side.

TIP
I use a cast iron tortilla press for this recipe. It cuts down on your prep time and gives you that perfect thickness every time!

CORN TORTILLAS

MAKES ABOUT 15 TORTILLAS

1¾ cups **corn flour**

1 cup + 2 Tbsp. **hot water**

½ tsp. **salt**

1. Stir together all of your ingredients in a large bowl. Knead until dough is smooth. Cover with a damp towel and allow to rest for 1 hour.

2. Divide your dough into 15 equal-sized pieces. Place between two pieces of parchment and roll thin.

3. Cook on a heated cast iron skillet for 30 seconds on each side.

TIP
I like to use a cast iron tortilla press for these to keep them thin and perfectly rounded.

BEEF TACOS

Taco tuesday is one we look forward to every week, and these easy beef tacos are the perfect way to celebrate!

SERVES 4

1 lb. **ground beef**

½ **onion**, chopped

1 clove **garlic**

1 cup **tomato sauce**

1 tsp. **chili powder**

½ tsp. **salt**

¼ tsp. **pepper**

Shredded cheese, salsa, sour cream, and other toppings

1. Add the ground beef and onion to a 10-inch skillet. Cook until meat is browned and onion is translucent. Stir in garlic and cook 1 minute more.

2. Stir in the tomato sauce, chili powder, salt, and pepper. Simmer 10 minutes.

3. Serve in flour or corn tortillas with desired toppings.

CRISPY CHICKEN STRIPS

There are a lot of perks to growing up close to family. One of my favorites was waiting for my Aunt to pull into the driveway of her home (which happened to be just across the street) and yelling from our screen door "Are you having CHICKEN??" I'm sure she made this recipe for me more than she wanted to but it was, and still is, one of my favorites. Simple and delicious. Thank you, Donna, for this amazing recipe.

SERVES 4

2 **chicken breasts**, sliced into strips

Seasoning salt

4 cups **rice cereal** (I use Rice Krispies)

1 cup **flour**

3 **eggs**, beaten

2-4 cups **oil**

1. Sprinkle both sides of your chicken with the seasoning salt.

2. Add your cereal to a blender. Pulse until powdered.

3. Create a dipping station by pouring your flour, eggs, and cereal into individual bowls. Dip each chicken strip into flour followed by the eggs and cereal.

4. Fill a 12-inch skillet with 1 inch of oil. Heat over medium-high heat until a drop of water sizzles. Add your chicken strips, being careful not to overcrowd. Cook until your chicken reaches an internal temperature of 165 degrees, making sure to flip halfway through.

BALSAMIC ROASTED CHERRY TOMATOES

If you've never had a roasted tomato you are missing out! My family lives for tomato season and is always looking for new and creative ways to enjoy the fresh fruit. Roasting releases the natural sweetness which pairs perfectly with balsamic. Enjoy on their own or on top of soft cheese and toast.

SERVES 2

1 Tbsp. **balsamic vinegar**

1–2 Tbsp. **olive oil**

1 pint **cherry tomatoes**

Pinch of **salt and pepper**

3 fresh **basil leaves**, sliced

1. Preheat your oven to 400 degrees.

2. Whisk together the balsamic vinegar and olive oil. Toss the cherry tomatoes to coat and spread into a single layer into a 10-inch cast iron pan.

3. Sprinkle with salt and pepper and bake 15 minutes.

4. Serve with fresh basil.

TIP
Adjust the flavor by swapping salt for garlic salt or trying fun flavors of balsamic!

INDIAN CHILI

I had to beg my mom to let me include this in the cast iron line-up. It's one of those super secret family recipes that is carefully guarded. It's so simple but brings a great punch of flavor and always brings everyone to the table.

SERVES 4

2 **pork chops**, medium thickness sliced into cubes

1½ tsp. **garlic salt**

1¼ cup **flour**, divided

¼–½ cup **oil**

½ tsp. **salt**

¼ tsp. **pepper**

1 can **pinto beans**, undrained

1 can diced **green chilies**

1–2 Tbsp. diced **jalapeños**

1–2 cups **water**

1. Season your pork with the garlic salt. Toss the pork in 1 cup of flour until lightly coated.

2. Heat oil in a deep 10-inch skillet. Add flour-covered meat and cook until browned. Remove the pork from the pan and set aside for later.

3. Whisk remaining ½ cup flour into the oil along with the salt and pepper. Cook 2–3 minutes.

4. Stir in the pinto beans, green chilies, jalapenos, and pork. Heat until just boiling.

5. Serve with warm tortillas and sliced potatoes.

SLICED POTATOES

These sliced potatoes have a beautiful presentation and are incredibly simple. Perfect side to any meal.

SERVES 4-5

4 **potatoes**

4 Tbsp. **butter**, melted

1 tsp. **salt**

½ tsp. **garlic powder**

4 Tbsp. shredded **cheddar cheese**

Chives

1. Wash potatoes. Slice them vertically into thin slices making sure not to cut all the way through. Place in a 10-inch cast iron pan and slightly fan.

2. Brush each potato with the melted butter and sprinkle with salt and garlic powder.

3. Bake at 425 degrees for 50 minutes.

4. Sprinkle with cheese and chives. Bake an additional 10 minutes or until cheese is melted.

BAKED BEAN CHILI

Baked beans give this chili a surprisingly sweet flavor that will win over everyone in the family! Super simple to make and perfect to fill your belly on cold winter nights!

SERVES 5

- 1 lb. **ground beef**
- ½ medium **onion**, chopped
- 2 (13.6-oz.) cans **Baked Beans**
- 1 can **diced tomatoes with chilies**
- 1½ cups **tomato juice**
- 1 envelope **chili seasoning**

1. Add your ground beef and onion in a 9-inch preheated skillet. Cook until the meat is browned and the onion is soft.

2. Add the remaining ingredients and simmer 10 minutes. Serve with shredded cheese, sour cream, chopped onions, or any of your other favorite chili toppings!

TIPS

Make sure you buy quality baked beans since that is where a majority of the flavor will come from.

Enjoy with a side of my cornbread found on page 78!

CORNBREAD

My go-to comfort food? Chili and cornbread! Once you give this recipe a try, you will toss out those box mixes! Easy and in the oven in less than ten minutes.

SERVES 8-10

1 cup **flour**

1 cup **cornmeal**

½ cup **sugar**

1 tsp. **salt**

3½ tsp. **baking powder**

1 egg

1 cup **milk**

⅓ cup **vegetable oil**

1. Preheat your oven to 400 degrees.

2. Whisk together your flour, cornmeal, sugar, salt, and baking powder in a large bowl. Stir in the egg, milk, and oil until fully combined. Pour into a 9-inch cast iron skillet.

3. Bake 20–25 minutes or until a toothpick comes out clean.

CINNAMON HONEY BUTTER

While this isn't technically a cast iron recipe, it's one you need to make! This butter holds a very special place in my heart (and stomach). It's sweet perfection that pairs wonderfully with any muffin or cornbread!

SERVES 8-10

1 cup **salted butter**, softened

6 Tbsp. **honey**

½ tsp. **cinnamon**

1. Whisk all ingredients with an electric mixer.

2. Serve on your favorite bread.

POT PIE

Every winter I get the request for my famous pot pie. I'm here to tell you my big secret: it's incredibly simple to make and packed with flavor. All you need is 20 minutes of prep time and you're on your way to a flavorful dish!

SERVES 6

5 Tbsp. **butter**

⅓ cup **flour**

½ tsp. **salt**

¼ tsp. **pepper**

2 cups **chicken broth**

¼ cup **whole milk**

2-3 cups cooked **chopped chicken**

2 cups **mixed vegetables ***

1 **pie crust**

1. Melt the butter in a deep 9-inch cast iron pan. Whisk in the flour and cook 3 minutes. Season with salt and pepper.

2. Slowly add the chicken broth, while continuing to whisk, along with the milk. Simmer until slightly thickened. Stir in the chicken and vegetables.

3. Top with your prepared pie crust. Cut two to three slits in the top to allow steam to escape during the cooking.

4. Bake 30–40 minutes or until golden.

TIPS

*I use frozen vegetable blends for this recipe.

For quicker prep, try using rotisserie chicken.

PIE CRUST

Keep this recipe on hand for pot pies or Thanksgiving desserts! Easy and delicious every time.

SERVES 6

1¼ cup **flour**

¼ tsp. **salt**

½ cup **butter**, cut into Tbsp. cubes

⅓ cup **ice cold water**

1. Whisk together the flour and salt.

2. Cut in the butter until your mixture resembles coarse crumbs.

3. Slowly stir in the water until your dough starts to come together.

4. Roll into a 10–12-inch circle and place into your pie pan. Trim the edges and use a fork to give them a nice edge. Use a fork to poke holes along the bottom of your crust to prevent bubbles.

5. Bake your crust according to the directions in your pie recipe.

TIP
The secret to a flaky crust is to keep your dough chilled during the mixing process. Make sure you take a break and refrigerate if the butter starts to melt.

CHEESESTEAK SKILLET

Cheesesteak lovers, let's take a second to appreciate just how amazing this recipe is. It's a one-pan pasta that combines all of the flavors of the classic sandwich into a super simple 30-minute recipe!

SERVES 6

1½ lbs. **ribeye steak**, sliced into thin strips

½ tsp. **salt**

¼ tsp. **pepper**

1 **onion**, thinly sliced

1 **green pepper**, thinly sliced

1 lb. box **pasta shells**

3½ cups **beef broth**

1 can **golden mushroom soup**

½ cup **sour cream**

4 oz. **cream cheese**

½ cup shredded **pepper jack cheese***

1. Heat a dutch oven over medium heat.

2. Season your steak with salt and pepper. Add to your dutch oven and cook until browned. Remove the meat from the pan, cover, and set aside.

3. Stir together your onion, pepper, pasta, broth, and mushroom soup in that same dutch oven. Bring to a simmer and cook 15 minutes, or until the pasta and vegetables are tender.

4. Add the meat back to the pan along with the sour cream and cream cheese. Heat to just a simmer. Top with pepper jack cheese and serve.

TIPS

Ask the meat counter to slice your steak for you. This will save you time when you're ready to get cooking!

*Substitute pepper jack cheese with cheddar or provolone for a different flavor.

BRUSCHETTA CHICKEN

Dinner for two ready in under an hour? Yes, please! This is mine and my husband's go-to date night recipe that is made time and time again. Simple, tasty, and topped with our favorite veggie!

SERVES 2

2 small **chicken breasts**

3 Tbsp. **Sun Dried tomato salad dressing**, divided

1 **roma tomato**, chopped

¼ cup shredded **mozzarella or parmesan cheese**

2 Tbsp. chopped **fresh basil**

1. Place the chicken and 2 tablespoons of dressing in a 9-inch cast iron pan. Make sure you turn the chicken to coat.

2. Preheat your oven to 350 degrees. Cook your chicken for 15 minutes.

3. While that is cooking stir together your tomato, cheese, basil, and remaining dressing in a small bowl.

4. Flip your chicken and cover with your tomato mixture. Cook an additional 8–10 minutes, or until the chicken reaches 165 degrees.

LEMON-BAKED CHICKEN

Everyone has a go-to meal they keep on hand. This is ours. We love how simple and yet tasty this chicken is! Bonus that your veggie is cooked right along with the main course making this one pot dinner a must for busy weeknights!

SERVES 4

1 Tbsp. **oil**

2 **chicken breasts**, halved

½ tsp. **salt**

¼ tsp. **pepper**

2 Tbsp. **garlic**, minced

½ bunch **asparagus**, ends trimmed

1 **lemon**, sliced

⅓ cup **chicken broth**

2 Tbsp. **lemon juice**

1–1½ tsp. **oregano**

1 tsp. **thyme**

1. Place a 12-inch skillet in your oven and preheat to 350 degrees. Once the oven has reached the proper temperature place the skillet on the stove top over medium heat and add the oil.

2. Season your chicken with the salt and pepper and place in your skillet. Cook two minutes and flip.

3. Add the garlic, asparagus, and lemon slices. In a separate bowl, combine all remaining ingredients to create the sauce.

4. Cover everything with the sauce and bake 10 minutes or until the chicken reaches 165 degrees.

JALAPEÑO POPPER DIP

Every year my in-laws throw a massive Super Bowl party. Everyone takes a treat or side to share and we try to get super creative. This dip was what we brought to the table way back in 2012. It disappeared so quickly that we were barely even able to try it!

SERVES 4-6

4 oz. **cream cheese**

¼ cup **mayonnaise**

3 Tbsp. **sharp cheddar cheese**

2 Tbsp. diced **pickled jalapeños**

1 Tbsp. diced **green chilies**

1 Tbsp. shredded **Parmesan cheese**

2 slices of **bacon**, cooked and crumbled

1. Preheat your oven to 350 degrees

2. Mix the cream cheese, mayonnaise, 2 tablespoons cheddar, jalapenos, chilies, parmesan, and half of the bacon in a medium bowl.

3. Transfer to a 5-inch cast iron skillet. Sprinkle with remaining cheese and bacon and bake 20 minutes.

CHICKEN ENCHILADAS

It's always nice to have an easy stand-by recipe and this is exactly that for me. It takes less than 10 minutes to put these easy enchiladas together, and they are kid approved!

SERVES 4-6

3 cups shredded **chicken**

1 cup shredded **sharp cheddar cheese**

1 cup **sour cream**

¼ **red onion**, diced

½ tsp. **salt**

¼ tsp. **pepper**

8 oz. of your favorite **enchilada sauce**

6 **tortillas**

1 cup shredded **pepper jack cheese**

Fresh **salsa**

1. Preheat your oven to 350 degrees.

2. Mix the chicken, sharp cheddar cheese, sour cream, red onion, salt, and pepper in a medium bowl.

3. Divide the chicken mixture between your tortillas. Roll and place in a 12-inch skillet.

4. Pour the enchilada sauce over your tortillas making sure to cover each one fully. Loosely cover with foil and bake 40 minutes.

5. Remove the foil, sprinkle with pepper jack cheese, and bake 10 minutes.

6. Serve with salsa.

APPLE-BAKED PORK CHOPS

I was driving down the street one fall afternoon when I stumbled across the most adorable apple orchard. They had just painted a giant red sign that read "Pick your own apples!" and who could pass that up? An hour later I was leaving with a enough of the little fruit to feed a small army. We started getting creative in the kitchen which lead to this family favorite. The tartness of the apple gives the pork the most amazing flavor!

SERVES 3

1 Tbsp. **oil**

3 boneless **pork chops**

Salt and pepper

½ **onion**. sliced

1 cup **water**

¼ cup **butter**

1 box **pork stuffing**, unprepared

1 medium **granny smith apple**, sliced

2 Tbsp. **brown sugar**

1. Preheat your oven to 350 degrees. Heat a large cast iron over medium heat with the oil.

2. Season your pork chops with salt and pepper on each side and add to the hot oil along with the onions. Cook until just browned on each side (about 2 minutes per side).

3. Remove the pork chops and onion and set aside.

4. Stir the water and butter together in your pan and bring to a boil. Add your packaged stuffing and onions and stir to combine. Top with the pork chops.

5. Toss the apples with the brown sugar and sprinkle over the top of your dish. Bake 20–30 minutes or until your pork chops are cooked completely.

DESSERTS

SKILLET BROWNIE

Dear fellow brownie lovers, this one is for you. Its chocolaty goodness is perfect for your sweet tooth and probably my favorite dessert in this book!

DESSERTS

1 cup **butter**, softened

¾ cup **granulated sugar**

¾ cup **brown sugar**

1 Tbsp. **vanilla extract**

3 **eggs**

¾ cup **cocoa powder**

1 cup **flour**

½ tsp. **baking powder**

¼ tsp. **salt**

1. Preheat your oven to 350 degrees.

2. Cream together the butter with both sugars. Add the vanilla and eggs and stir until combined.

3. In a separate bowl, whisk together the cocoa, flour, baking powder, and salt. Stir into the wet ingredients.

4. Divide into five 3½-inch skillets. Bake 25 minutes or until a toothpick comes out clean.

CHERRY DUMP CAKE

This is another great one from my grandma. All you need are a few simple ingredients and you have a decadent dessert ready to serve!

DESSERTS

1 (21-oz.) can **cherry pie filling**

1 cup **white cake mix**

6 Tbsp. **butter**

1. Preheat your oven to 350 degrees.

2. Spread the pie filling into a 10-inch skillet. Sprinkle the cake mix over the top.

3. Cut your butter into small pieces and place over the top of the cake.

4. Bake 45 minutes or until golden brown.

CHOCOLATE CHIP SKILLET COOKIE

Years ago my husband took me to a little hole-in-the-wall pizza place for dinner and the first thing he did was pre order their skillet cookie. This is a big deal for him since he really is not a dessert fan, but when they brought out our treat I instantly fell in love and knew it would need to be recreated. Since then we have enjoyed our own version as a family favorite!

½ cup **butter**

¼ cup **brown sugar**

¼ cup **sugar**

1 **egg**

1 tsp. **vanilla**

1 cup **flour**

½ tsp. **baking soda**

¼ tsp. **salt**

½ cup **semi-sweet chocolate chips**

1. Preheat your oven to 325 degrees.

2. Add your butter to a 8-inch skillet and heat until melted. Stir in both sugars and cook until glossy.

3. Remove from the heat and allow to cool to room temperature. Stir in the eggs, vanilla, flour, baking soda, salt, and chocolate chips.

4. Bake 30 minutes.

TIP
I love serving these cookies with ice cream.

CAKE MIX PEACH COBBLER

This peach cobbler gets a special shout out to my brother and sister in-law. They introduced me to this delicious cheat recipe and we've made it a dozen times since then.

1 box **yellow cake mix**

2 (30-oz.) cans **peaches**, drained

1 can **Sprite**

1. Preheat your oven to 350 degrees.

2. Mix all three ingredients in a dutch oven. Bake 35 minutes or until a toothpick comes out clean.

3. Serve with ice cream.

TIP
I suggest using an enamel-lined pan for this one to avoid sticking.

CINNAMON ROLLS

My son had one request for this book, cinnamon rolls. When you bake this fun treat in cast iron you get a beautiful caramelized bread that has an out of this world flavor. You will never go back to the traditional pan method again.

¼ oz. **active yeast** pack

½ cup **warm water**

½ cup **milk**

¼ cup **sugar**

6 Tbsp. **butter**, melted

1 tsp. **salt**

1 large **egg**

3½ cups **all-purpose flour**

FILLING

1 cup **brown sugar**

1 Tbsp. **cinnamon**

⅛ tsp. **salt**

½ cup **butter**, soft

FROSTING

2 Tbsp. **butter**

1 cup **powdered sugar**

½ tsp. **pure vanilla extract**

1-3 Tbsp. **milk**

1. Sprinkle your yeast over your water in a small bowl. Set aside and allow to sit for at least 5 minutes.

2. Combine the milk, sugar, butter, salt, and egg in the bowl of an electric mixer. Stir to combine. Add 2 cups of flour and stir until fully incorporated. Stir in the yeast mixture. Add the remaining flour and knead 5–10 minutes or until smooth.

3. Transfer your dough to a greased bowl. Cover with a clean towel and allow to rise until doubled in size (1–2 hours).

4. Turn your dough out onto a lightly floured surface. Roll into a 15×9 inch rectangle. Spread ½ cup soft butter across the dough. Whisk together the brown sugar, salt, and cinnamon. Sprinkle over your butter. Roll, starting on the long end, to form a large log. Cut into 15 pieces.

5. Place your rolls into a 12-inch cast iron pan. Cover with plastic wrap and place in the refrigerator overnight.

6. In the morning, place the cinnamon rolls in the oven without turning it on. Let them come to room temperature and slightly rise for 45 minutes to 1 hour. Remove from the oven and preheat to 350 degrees.

7. Bake 25 minutes or until slightly browned.

8. Whisk together the frosting ingredients and spread over the top. Serve alongside your favorite breakfast recipes.

CHERRY CRUMBLE

My love for cherries has always run deep. Growing up my grandparents would often take us to visit a local cherry farm to pick some of the sweet little gems. While we would leave with bucket fulls, I'm sure even more made their way straight into my stomach. This crumble was my grandmother's recipe and one I enjoy to this day!

2 cups **dark sweet cherries** (thawed if frozen)

⅓ cup **granulated sugar**

½ cup + 1 Tbsp. **flour**

½ tsp. **almond extract**

3 Tbsp. **salted butter**, melted

¼ cup **rolled oats**

3 Tbsp. **brown sugar**

1. Preheat your oven to 425 degrees.

2. Mix your cherries with the granulated sugar, 1 tablespoon flour, and almond extract. Spread into an 8-inch cast iron skillet that has been greased with either butter or non stick spray.

3. Combine the remaining ½ cup flour, butter, oats, and brown sugar in a small bowl. Mix until crumbled.

4. Sprinkle the mixture over the top of your cherries. Bake 40 minutes or until lightly browned.

SNICKERDOODLE BISCUITS

Your favorite cookie turned biscuits! These are an easy fun twist on the classic treat. Save that scrap dough from your morning biscuits for a homemade version or reach for the refrigerated biscuit dough!

2 Tbsp. **butter**

1 can **refrigerated biscuit dough**

½ cup **sugar**

1 Tbsp. **cinnamon**

1. Preheat your oven to 350 degrees.

2. Melt butter in a 12-inch pan.

3. While the butter is melting whisk together the sugar and cinnamon in a bowl.

4. Dip your biscuits in the sugar mixture and place in your prepared pan.

5. Bake according to the directions on the biscuit package.

6. Top warm biscuits with cinnamon honey butter.

BLUEBERRY PIE

Galette is the fancy name for a pie. We love to transform any of our favorite pie flavors into this beautifully folded treat. The presentation is divine and the mixture of almond and blueberry is sure to please the crowd!

SERVES 12

4 cups **blueberries**

¾ cup **sugar**

3 Tbsp. **cornstarch**

1 Tbsp. **fresh lemon juice**

½ tsp. **cinnamon**

¼ tsp. **almond extract**

1 **pie crust**

1 **egg**, beaten

1 Tbsp. **sugar**

1. Preheat the oven to 400 degrees.

2. In a large bowl, combine the blueberries, sugar, cornstarch, lemon juice, cinnamon, and almond extract. Stir gently to combine.

3. Place your pie crust in a 10-inch skillet. Using a slotted spoon, transfer the blueberries to the skillet.

4. Fold the edges of the pastry over the filling, leaving the center uncovered.

5. Brush the egg over the pastry, then sprinkle with the coarse sugar.

6. Bake the pie until the edges of the crust are golden brown and the filling is bubbling, 35–40 minutes.

APPLE CRISP

All of the fun flavors of fall are packed into this dessert. Serve alone or topped with a giant scoop of ice cream!

2 Tbsp. + ½ cup **butter**

6 **granny smith apples**, peeled and sliced

2 Tbsp. + 1 cup **brown sugar**

½ tsp. + 1 tsp. **cinnamon**

¾ cup **old fashioned oats**

¾ cup **flour**

1. Preheat your oven to 350 degrees.

2. Place 2 tablespoons of butter in a deep 9-inch skillet. Melt in the oven.

3. Toss your apples with 2 tablespoons of brown sugar and ½ teaspoon of cinnamon. Pour over the melted butter in the heated pan.

4. Mix together the remaining brown sugar and cinnamon with the oats and flour. Cut in the ½ cup butter with two knives or a pastry cutter. Sprinkle over the top of the apples. Bake 40 minutes.

INDEX

INDEX

COOKING MEASUREMENT EQUIVALENTS

CUPS	TABLESPOONS	FLUID OUNCES
$\frac{1}{8}$ cup	2 Tbsp.	1 fl. oz.
¼ cup	4 Tbsp.	2 fl. oz.
$\frac{1}{3}$ cup	5 Tbsp. + 1 tsp.	
½ cup	8 Tbsp.	4 fl. oz.
$\frac{2}{3}$ cup	10 Tbsp. + 2 tsp.	
¾ cup	12 Tbsp.	6 fl. oz.
1 cup	16 Tbsp.	8 fl. oz.

CUPS	FLUID OUNCES	PINTS/QUARTS/GALLONS
1 cup	8 fl. oz.	½ pint
2 cups	16 fl. oz.	1 pint = ½ quart
3 cups	24 fl. oz.	1½ pints
4 cups	32 fl. oz.	2 pints = 1 quart
8 cups	64 fl. oz.	2 quarts = ½ gallon
16 cups	128 fl. oz.	4 quarts = 1 gallon

Other Helpful Equivalents

1 Tbsp.	3 tsp.
8 oz.	½ lb.
16 oz.	1 lb.

METRIC MEASUREMENT EQUIVALENTS

Approximate Weight Equivalents

OUNCES	POUNDS	GRAMS
4 oz.	¼ lb.	113 g
5 oz.		142 g
6 oz.		170 g
8 oz.	½ lb.	227 g
9 oz.		255 g
12 oz.	¾ lb.	340 g
16 oz.	1 lb.	454 g

Approximate Volume Equivalents

CUPS	US FLUID OUNCES	MILLILITERS
⅛ cup	1 fl. oz.	30 ml
¼ cup	2 fl. oz.	59 ml
½ cup	4 fl. oz.	118 ml
¾ cup	6 fl. oz.	177 ml
1 cup	8 fl. oz.	237 ml

Other Helpful Equivalents

½ tsp.	2½ ml
1 tsp.	5 ml
1 Tbsp.	15 ml

NOTES

JESSECA HALLOWS

ABOUT THE AUTHOR

JESSECA HALLOWS is the recipe developer and photographer behind the popular website One Sweet Appetite. Her passion for food has driven her to create beautiful and tasty meals that the whole family will enjoy. Her work has been featured in online magazines as well as numerous news and media outlets. She lives and works near Salt Lake City, Utah, creating recipes for her site as well as major brands, including Kraft, Campbell's, Ghirardelli, and OXO.

SCAN to visit

WWW.ONESWEETAPPETITE.COM